# Unlikely Allies
## Monotheism and the Rise of Science

### Mark Worthing

**a.** Acorn Press

Published by Acorn Press
An imprint of Bible Society AustraliaACN 148 058 306 | Charity
licence 19 000 528
GPO Box 4161
Sydney NSW 2001
Australia
www.acornpress.net.au | www.biblesociety.org.au

© Mark Worthing, 2024. All rights reserved.

ISBN 978-0-647-53349-9

First published by Morning Star Publishing in 2019, ISBN 978-0-
648-45384-0

NATIONAL
LIBRARY
OF AUSTRALIA

A catalogue record for this
book is available from the
National Library of Australia

Cover and text design and layout by John Healy

# TONY MORGAN

"Unlikely Allies: Monotheism and the Rise of Natural Science" was the title of the inaugural Tony Morgan Lecture on Science, Faith, and Culture at New College, University of New South Wales on 5 June 2018. This book is an expanded version of that lecture.

Antony "Tony" Morgan (1940–2016) was an economist originally from Sydney. He spent most of his adult life in Canberra, working for the Commonwealth Government. He was an active member of St Andrew's Presbyterian Church in Canberra and an avid reader of theological literature. Tony was passionate about Christianity, engaging effectively and intellectually with contemporary Australian culture, and he read widely, especially in the areas of apologetics and the science and faith dialogue.

Toward the end of 2015, Tony decided to act on his passion for Christian engagement with the sciences and culture and find ways to support this work financially. One of the groups he had long been following was ISCAST. After initiating contact, meetings followed with Tony in Adelaide, Canberra, and Melbourne, which he greatly enjoyed. Tony had long conversations, especially with Chris Mulherin, Executive Director of ISCAST, and ISCAST fellow Mark Worthing about apologetics and the work of ISCAST. He decided to make a significant initial contribution to ISCAST to support Chris' role and to enable a greater focus on apologetics.

Tony wanted to do much more and to be a part of the lectures, training programs, conferences, and publications that were all a part of his vision. Sadly, he passed away suddenly in December 2016 before he could see his vision become a reality. As a part of his estate, Tony wished to contribute to ISCAST.

His family graciously carried out his wishes, and Tony's bequest is now being used for the very things Tony so passionately wanted to see happen. The *Science, Faith, and Culture* lectures are a part of that legacy. Tony would have been pleased that the lecture series established in his memory is to be held in his beloved home city of Sydney.

# ABSTRACT

In *Unlikely Allies: Monotheism and the Rise of Science,* the many claims by various religious communities that their tradition played a unique role in the rise of the natural sciences are reviewed. After a brief survey of these claims and the objections to them, it is argued that monotheism in general, more than any particular manifestation of it, played a significant role in the rise of modern science. The case for monotheism's positive role in the development of science is not based alone on the historical and geographic proximity of epochs of growth in the natural sciences and strong monotheistic intellectual communities. It is also based on the explanatory value of the proposition that certain key features of monotheism provided fertile conditions for the rise of the natural sciences. Christianity, while not solely responsible for producing these conditions, played a significant role in the rise of science in the modern era. Given these historical links, the view that religion—especially monotheistic religion—is the natural enemy of science must be rejected. Contrary to popular perception, belief in one God and the natural sciences have been unlikely allies for over two millennia.

# Contents

# INTRODUCTION

In recent years, a rather heated debate has arisen over the role that religion, and Christianity in particular, played in the rise of the natural sciences. The general consensus among historians of science is expressed by Peter Harrison:

> Could modern science have arisen outside the theological matrix of Western Christendom? It is difficult to say. What can be said for certain is that it did arise in that environment, and that theological ideas underpinned some of its central assumptions. Those who argue for the incompatibility of science and religion will draw little comfort from history.[1]

However, some proponents of the thesis that Christianity is responsible for the rise of science have sought to claim more than this. They have argued that Christianity itself has been the necessary and essential cause for the rise of science. In other words, they have argued that science would not have, and could not have, arisen apart from the foundation of Christian thinking. Most notable among those making this argument in recent years have been Dinesh D'Souza and Rodney Stark.[2] Their claims have gone beyond the more nuanced claims of most previous studies on the relationship between science and faith. Such views, as expected, provoked a response from those aligned with the New Atheist camp, particularly Richard Carrier and Jerry Coyne. They argued that the view that religion played a role in the rise of science is, at best, misguided. In fact,

---

1 Peter Harrison, "Christianity and the Rise of Western Science," (*ABC Religion and Ethics*, May 8, 2012) http://abc.net.au/religion/articles/2012/05/08.
2 See, for instance, Dinesh D'Souza, *What's So Great about Christianity* (Chicago: Tyndale, 2008); and Rodney Stark, *For the Glory of God. How Monotheism Led to Reformations, Science, Witch Hunts, and the End of Slavery* (Princeton, NJ: Princeton University Press, 2004).

they contend that religion played no positive role in the rise of science, but rather that religion, especially Christianity, has historically resisted science.[3]

So, who is right? As is often the case when strongly held views arise in opposition to one another, neither is entirely right—or wrong.

To introduce the contemporary debate over the influence of religion on the rise of science, I will share something of my own experience of science and faith as opposing forces. My early religious upbringing was as a conservative Protestant Christian. The natural sciences were openly viewed in a negative light and as a threat to religious belief. My view of science and religion may have been dichotomised, but it was clear and easy to understand. Science and Christian faith presented conflicting and mutually exclusive approaches to truth. As far as I understood, it was the one point on which religious leaders and scientists agreed: science and religion were natural adversaries. Like many young people from such a background, my worldview concerning science and religion began to unravel at university. It was unsettling to discover that foundational scientific theories such as Big Bang cosmology and the theory of evolution via natural selection had significant evidential support behind them. The discovery of the works of Pierre Teilhard de Chardin in my university library was initially baffling. How could a Christian theologian develop

---

3 See particularly Richard Carrier, "Christianity Was Not Responsible for Modern Science," in *The Christian Delusion. Why Faith Fails*, ed. John Loftus (Amherst, NY: Prometheus Books, 2010: 396–419); and Jerry Coyne, "Did Christianity (and other Religions) Promote the Rise of Science?" in a post from *Why Evolution Is True* (blog), October 18, 2013, who lists 11 reasons why Christianity cannot be said to have promoted the rise of science. At: https://whyevolutionistrue.wordpress.com/2013/10/18/did-christianity-and-other-religions-promote-the-rise-of-science/. Carrier's work is particularly *ad hominem*, with the motives, sanity, and credentials of his opponents all questioned. At one stage, he questions how Stark could maintain his teaching position with his views.

a view of God and creation that corresponded to the theory of evolution? But several weeks and volumes later, he had proved my salvation. If Teilhard could build an exposition of the Christian faith around an evolutionary worldview, perhaps science was not the enemy of faith. I soon came to understand that a serious commitment to belief in God as creator demanded a more than passing interest in the knowledge of the natural world;[4] how, then, did the idea arise that science and faith are natural adversaries?

---

4 Wolfhart Pannenberg, for instance, suggested that, "If the God of the Bible is creator of the universe, then it is not possible to understand fully or even appropriately the processes of nature without reference to that God. If, on the contrary, nature can be appropriately understood without reference to the God of the Bible then that God cannot be creator of the universe." Pannenberg, "Theological Questions to Scientists," in *The Sciences and Theology in the Twentieth Century*, ed. A. Peacocke (Notre Dame, IN: University of Notre Dame Press, 1981), 4.

## Part One

# A brief taxonomy of theories concerning the link between individual monotheistic traditions and the rise of science

## *Science arises despite opposition from religion: The Draper-White Thesis*

The view that science arose despite opposition from religion is essentially espoused by Richard Carrier, Jerry Coyne, and the New Atheists generally. However, its origins go back more than a century to the heat of the early debate over the work of Charles Darwin. The appearance of Charles Darwin's 1859 *The Origin of Species* had a profound if unintended impact on the relationship between Christian theology and the natural sciences.[1] The debate over Darwin's theory even gave rise to a re-construction of the history of the relationship between science and religion. This can be most clearly seen in John William Draper's *History of the Conflict between Religion and Science* (1875), and Andrew Dickson White's *A History of the Warfare of Science with Theology in Christendom* (1896). They portrayed the entire history of scientific development as a war against a bigoted and narrow-minded establishment (Christianity) that feared science and was being engulfed by its advance. Draper, warning of an intensified conflict between science and religion, concluded his book with the admonition:

> Faith must render an account of herself to Reason. Mysteries must give place to facts. Religion must relinquish that ...

_____

1 Cf. Mark Worthing, "Theology and Science – A Brief History," in *God and Science in Classroom and Pulpit*, revised edition, eds. G. Buxton, C. Mulherin, and M. Worthing (Melbourne: Morning Star, 2018), 92ff. The negative reaction to Darwin's theory among more conservative theologians was not immediate, with many of the best known evangelical theologians of the day publicly supportive of the theory. See, for instance, David Livingstone, *Darwin's Forgotten Defenders: The Encounter between Evangelical Theology and Evolutionary Thought* (Grand Rapids: Eerdmans, 1987).

domineering position which she has so long maintained against Science. ... The ecclesiastic must learn to keep himself within the domain he has chosen, and cease to tyrannize over the [natural] philosopher, who, conscious of his own strength and the purity of his motives, will bear such interference no longer.[2]

Even White, whose views were more moderate than those of Draper, painted the various conflicts between theology and science, both real and imagined, as one-sided affairs in which an aggressive and overbearing ecclesiastical structure continually sought to suppress a pure and truth-seeking science and its unassuming practitioners. In fact, building on Draper's earlier work, White felt that the conflict was portrayed too broadly as being between science and religion. White saw the heart of the conflict as between science and dogmatic theology. He felt that if religion could be wrested from the hands of dogmatic theology, and not meddle in areas of science, then it could contribute much that was useful to the human enterprise.[3]

Draper, in particular, portrayed both religion and science in such a selective way that he drew heavy and immediate criticism, especially (and not unexpectedly) from the side of theology. W. H. Jellie, in his review of the book, was especially concerned at the dichotomy of science and religion. He wrote:

A man may have been as devout a believer as Newton or Faraday, but his science is wrested from him and turned over to one camp, and his religion, as the foe of science, is necessarily turned over to the other. This may perhaps be called impartiality, or possibly, learning, but it seems to us the very mockery of argument, the reduction *ad absurdum* of the method pursued by Dr Draper. ...We protest then against the misrepresentations of Dr Draper. It is not creditable to his learning, if he did not know the

2 John William Draper, *History of the Conflict Between Religion and Science* (London: Henry S. King, 1875), 367.
3 Andrew Dickson White, *A History of the Warfare of Science with Theology*

facts. It is discreditable to his impartiality if he marshalled them in such a way, by bringing some in the foreground, and keeping others in the background, as to leave a false impression.[4]

Despite their shortcomings, these books had a significant impact. As James Moore has written, "if Draper's *History* was inadequate, those who read it were inadequately equipped to judge it." Draper's work appealed to many scientists of the day "because it flattered the growing faith in the omnicompetence of science, in the power and prerogative of scientists to embrace all of life within the framework of 'law.'"[5]

The warfare model of Draper and White had far-reaching consequences. Out of this model, for instance, arose the still popular view that the astronomer Copernicus held back publication of his *De Revolutionibus*, which outlines his heliocentric theory of the universe, out of fear of persecution by the church. In fact, Copernicus, himself a minor church official, had already outlined his views years before his death in his brief *Commentariolus*. The only pressure that Copernicus appears to have received from church officials came from several members of the Lutheran University of Wittenberg (where Martin Luther was at the time teaching) and from Cardinal Schönberg in a letter to Copernicus dated November 1536. Both sources urged him to publish a full account of his theory so that it could be studied.[6] Fred Hoyle, no friend himself of organised religion, conceded, "the factors which

---

*in Christendom*, 2 vols. (New York: D. Appleton and Company, 1896), vol. 1, ix-xii.

4 W. H. Jellie, "Draper's 'Religion and Science'," in *Dickinson's Theological Quarterly* 3, (1877): 153.

5 James Moore, *The Post-Darwinian Controversies. A Study of the Protestant Struggle To Come to Terms with Darwin in Great Britain and America 1870–1900* (Cambridge: Cambridge University Press, 1979), 21.

6 Cf. Mark Worthing, *God, Creation, and Contemporary Physics* (Minneapolis: Fortress Press, 1996), 9ff.

deterred Copernicus [from publication] must either have been scientific or were personal to himself."[7] However, the image persists of a revolutionary astronomer who was fearful of the church's reaction to his theory.

The Galileo affair, the actual details of which are embarrassing enough to the church, was also reinterpreted. Ignored was the personal conflict between Galileo and his one-time supporter, Pope Urban VIII, as well as Galileo's pro-Spanish connections at a time when Spain was putting pressure on the papacy. Significantly, little attention was given to the fact that Galileo was so frustrated by the Pope's arguments against the Copernican theory, put to him in private conversation, that he put these arguments into the mouth of the fool Simplicius in his next book.[8] The complex factors surrounding Galileo's condemnation by the church went well beyond his support for heliocentrism.

Most intriguing of all was the success of the attempt to credit the church with the medieval superstition of the masses that the Earth was flat. Indeed, even today many scientists and theologians caution against a return to the days in which the church held to the idea of a flat Earth. The only problem is that neither the church nor any of its recognised teachers ever held to the idea of a flat Earth.[9] Medieval diagrams of the world consistently portrayed it as a circle, and philosophy and theology texts alike spoke of it as round or as a sphere.[10]

---

7 Fred Hoyle, *Nicolas Copernicus: An Essay on His Life and Work* (London: Heinemann, 1973), 32–33.

8 Cf. Maurice Finocchiaro, "Myth 8: That Galileo Was Imprisoned and Tortured for Advocating Copernicanism," in *Galileo Goes to Jail and Other Myths about Science and Faith*, ed. Ronald Numbers (Cambridge, MA: Harvard University Press, 2009), 68ff.; and Mark Worthing, *God, Creation and Contemporary Physics*, 11ff.

9 With the possible exception of a monk named Cosmas who wrote a treatise in 535 on "Christian Topography." See Whitehead, *Science and the Modern World* (Cambridge: Cambridge University Press, 1933), 225–226.

10 Lesley Cormack, "Myth 3: That Medieval Christians Taught That the

Despite the often-poor documentation and obvious prejudice of the Draper-White thesis, as well as its eventual rejection by most respected historians of religion and science, it contained enough truth to sustain its influence and colour, to this day, the view of many in both scientific and religious communities. Further impetus for this view was provided by the rise of Young Earth Creationism, beginning especially with the appearance of Henry Morris and John Whitcomb's *The Genesis Flood* in 1961.[11] Advocates of this view formed an odd alliance with non-religious proponents of the Draper-White thesis. For the emerging Young Earth Creationist movement, science and faith were also natural enemies that had always been in conflict. However, in this version of the story, it was science that suppressed the intellectual freedom of religion.

The Draper-White thesis has found scant historical support. However, could the opposite case be made? Could religion, especially monotheism, have actually played a positive role in the development of science? Thomas Kuhn, in his seminal work *The Structure of Scientific Revolutions*, pointed out that growth in scientific theories often comes in revolutions rather than through incremental progress.[12] While Kuhn's ideas are not without their difficulties,[13] they provide an important

Earth Was Flat," in Numbers, *Galileo Goes to Jail*, 28ff.

11 Cf. Ronald Numbers, *The Creationists: The Evolution of Scientific Creationism* (New York: Alfred Knopf, 1992), 184ff.; and Michael Ruse, *The Evolution-Creation Struggle* (Cambridge, MA: Harvard University Press, 2006), 129ff.

12 Thomas Kuhn, *The Structure of Scientific Revolutions*, 2nd enlarged ed. (Chicago: University of Chicago Press, 1970), 160ff. Edwin El-Mahassni, among others, has pointed out that Kuhn's insight into how science often progresses through revolutions (which he likened to political revolutions and even to religious conversions) when an old paradigm is rejected for a new one, is not dissimilar to how Christian faith has developed in its doctrinal expression. See also Edwin El-Mahassni, "Kuhn's Structural Revolutions and the Development of Christian Doctrine: A Systematic Discussion," *Heythrop Journal*, February 15, 2017.

13 Cf. for instance A. F. Chalmers, *What Is This Thing Called Science?* 3rd

insight into how science progresses. One might argue that the growth of science as a whole, and not just the individual theories within it, has followed this same pattern. With this in mind, we note that the most significant epochs of growth in science have been associated with periods, regions, and individuals with strong monotheistic faith commitments.[14] Is this merely coincidental, or does the historical evidence suggest that monotheism somehow helped give rise to modern science and the research culture associated with it? If this is the case, is it monotheism in general or only particular manifestations of monotheism that played a key role in the evolution of science? The following survey, a meta-study of many studies focused on the role played by individual religious traditions in the rise of science, indicates that there is strong evidence for a significant relationship between natural science and religion, especially monotheistic religion.

### Science arose out of Puritan England

Many of these studies have been very specific in their focus. Between 1938 and 1975 at least three separate monographs appeared arguing that modern science owed its origins not just to religion, not just to monotheism, not just to Christianity, not just to Protestantism, not just to Reformed Protestantism, but specifically to English Protestant Puritanism.[15] A fourth work, R. Hooykaas' classic *Religion and the Rise of Modern Science*, gave attention to the role of the English Puritans but argued that modern science owed its inception to Calvinism more generally

---

ed. (Brisbane: University of Queensland Press, 1999), 119ff.

14 As Jaki observed, "monotheism was an unquestioned tenet in Cordova as well as in Constantinople, in Baghdad as well as in Rome, in Cairo as well as in Paris." (*The Road of Science and the Ways to God*, 35.)

15 Cf. Robert K. Merton, *Science, Technology, and Society in 17th-Century England* (Bruges: St Catherine Press, 1938); Christopher Hill, *The Intellectual Origins of the English Revolution* (Oxford: Clarendon Press, 1965); and Charles Webster, *The Great Instauration: Science, Medicine and Reform 1626–1660* (London: Duckworth, 1975).

and the so-called Protestant work ethic particularly. This view is commonly referred to as "the Merton thesis" as it was put forward most prominently and strongly by Thomas Merton in his 1938 book *Science, Technology, and Society in 17th-Century England*, which was based on his 1936 doctoral thesis.[16]

In short, the Merton thesis has two parts. The first part of his thesis belongs more properly to the philosophy of science and holds that science changes due to an accumulation of observations along with improvements in scientific techniques and methodology. The second part of the thesis, which belongs more properly to the history of science, is the one that is of particular interest for our current study. Merton sees the height of scientific achievement and advance as having taken place in England in the seventeenth century. He then moves to establish a correlation between the strong Puritan influences at that time (including their work ethic and scientific values) and the scientific revolution of the seventeenth and eighteenth centuries.

It is true that there were many significant contributions coming out of seventeenth-century England. Many of these individuals, not surprisingly, had a Puritan influence, as evidenced by the strong Puritan representation among the founding members of the Royal Society of London in 1660.[17] However, other Christians could be forgiven for thinking that too much was being claimed by the Merton thesis.

### Science arose out of the Protestant Reformation
Others have argued more broadly that Protestantism in general laid the foundations for the rise of modern science.[18] Luther

---

16 R. Hooykaas, *Religion and the Rise of Modern Science* (Edinburgh: Scottish Academic Press, 1972).

17 As Ian Barbour points out, seven out of ten founding members of the Royal Society were Puritans, and many of these were clergy. Barbour, *Religion and Science: Historical and Contemporary Issues*, revised and expanded ed. (London: SCM Press, 1998), 25.

18 Cf. for instance Harold Nebelsick, *The Renaissance, the Reformation*

already expressed favourable views toward the natural sciences as independent disciplines in the early sixteenth century, and his colleagues at the University of Wittenberg included some of Copernicus' earliest supporters.[19] Despite some rather embarrassing medieval beliefs, including the spontaneous generation of mice and dung beetles and his view that birds survived the winter frozen in icy waters, Luther was clear that the study of nature had merit in its own right and was to be independent of the study of theology.[20]

The Swiss Reformer John Calvin also expressed views that can be considered supportive of scientific endeavour. In his *Institutes of the Christian Religion* he wrote:

> There are innumerable evidences both in heaven and on earth that declare his wonderful wisdom; not only those more recondite matters for the closer observation of which astronomy, medicine, and all natural science are intended, but also those which thrust themselves upon the sight of even the most untutored and ignorant persons.[21]

If, according to Calvin, the pursuit of science can witness to the glory of God, then scientific ability must be seen as a gift from God, even when such gifts are manifest in those who do not believe in God. Calvin asked,

> Shall we say that they are insane who developed medicine, devoting their labor to our benefit? What shall we say of all the mathematical sciences? Shall we consider them the

---

*and the Rise of Science* (Edinburgh: T&T Clark, 1992) who argued that the Reformation "opened up people's minds for modern science" but was at pains to point out that Reformation theology alone did not have "a monopoly influence in this direction" (159). See also R. Hooykaas, *Religion and the Rise of Modern Science* (Edinburgh: Scottish Academic Press, 1972).

19 Cf. David Knight, *Copernicus* (London: Franklin Watts, 1965), 192–193.

20 See the chapter "Luther on the Border of Superstition and Science," in M. Worthing, *Martin Luther. A Wild Boar in the Lord's Vineyard* (Melbourne: Morning Star, 2017), 141ff.

21 John Calvin, *Institutes of the Christian Religion*, trans. F. L. Battles (Philadelphia: Westminster Press, 1960), 201 (1.16.3).

ravings of madmen? No, we cannot read the writings of the ancients on these subjects without great admiration.

He further argued,

> If the Lord had willed that we be helped in physics, dialectic, mathematics, and other like disciplines, by the work and ministry of the ungodly, let us use this assistance. For if we neglect God's gifts freely offered in these arts, we ought to suffer just punishment for our sloths.[22]

R. Hooykaas, in his classic text *Religion and the Rise of Modern Science*, is sympathetic to the Merton thesis but wants to broaden this to include Reformation Protestantism more generally. He begins by pointing out that Protestants were disproportionately represented in early scientific societies, especially the Académie des Sciences in Paris. He suggests some of the beliefs and traits of Protestants of that era that could explain their high level of interest and involvement in the sciences. Doctrinally, he focused on the teachings on predestination, i.e., the belief that the chief end of humanity is to glorify God (question one in the Westminster Catechism) and the belief in the priesthood of all believers.[23] Hooykaas also felt there was a special appreciation among Protestants for the Bible as a source for science. However, the role of the Bible among Protestant scientists may have had much more to do with exegetical methodology than as a source for scientific ideas.

Peter Harrison, in *The Bible, Protestantism and the Rise of Natural Science*, argued that the Protestant emphasis on the study and exegesis of sacred texts laid down a methodology that led to scientific investigation of the natural world.[24] This theory, not surprisingly, was more acceptable to most

---

22 Calvin, *Institutes of the Christian Religion*, 274ff (2.2.15–16).
23 Hooykaas, *Religion and the Rise of Modern Science* (Edinburgh: Scottish Academic Press), 98–101, 105–114.
24 Cf. Peter Harrison, *The Bible, Protestantism, and the Rise of Natural Science* (Cambridge: Cambridge University Press, 1998).

Protestants than the English-Puritan theory. It also signalled that the science historian pursuing this line of research should be looking not for what was unique to English Puritanism but for what was unique to Protestantism.

A classic examination of the relationship between Protestantism and the natural sciences is John Dillenberger's 1961 *Protestant Thought and Natural Science.* Dillenberger was well aware that prominent twentieth-century theologians such as Karl Barth and Paul Tillich, influenced by existentialism, did not often positively engage with the natural sciences. Regardless, they managed to produce approaches that allowed both the sciences and theology to undergo significant revolutions in thought. In meeting the impact of thinkers from Galileo to Darwin head on, Barth and Tillich put theology "in a position of new openness," no longer "having to be an opponent to a doctrinaire science and hence, becoming doctrinaire itself."[25] This was freeing and ultimately positive for both the sciences and theology.

For all the many books and discussions about the role played by Protestant theology in the rise of modern science, the story of the historical relationship between science and faith cannot be adequately covered by examining Protestant contributions alone. Indeed, it became apparent that many advances in science could be traced to times and places in which Protestantism had no influence.

### *Science arose out of Medieval and Renaissance Catholicism*
A case can also be made that modern science finds its origins in medieval and Renaissance Roman Catholicism. This view points to the impact of the monastery and cathedral schools, which taught medicine and natural philosophy as well as theology, and out of which the early European universities

---

25 John Dillenberger, *Protestant Thought and Natural Science. A Historical Study* (London: Collins, 1961), 262ff.

grew. It suggests that Albertus Magnus and Thomas Aquinas played an important role in adapting Aristotelian philosophy to Christian thought. It reminds us that Copernicus and Galileo, among others, were part of the Roman church and that the first scientific society was Roman Catholic and predated the foundation of the Royal Society by more than half a century. This view was put forward in the early part of the twentieth century by the philosopher Alfred North Whitehead. He claimed that "faith in the possibility of science, generated antecedently to the development of modern scientific theory, is an unconscious derivative from medieval theology." Whitehead highlights the influence of two sixth-century Latin theologians, St Benedict and Gregory the Great, who contributed to the reconstruction of Europe, including "a more effective scientific mentality than that of the ancient world."[26]

## Science arose out of the Christian West, both Protestant and Catholic

Roman Catholics played an early and important role in the development of modern science in Europe. Copernicus was a minor cleric who died in good standing with the church, and Galileo, despite his disputes with the hierarchy of the church, never saw himself as anything but a Roman Catholic Christian. The first known scientific society founded in Christian Europe was not the Royal Society of London in 1660, but the Italian Catholic Lincean Academy founded in 1603. While seventeenth-century Puritans were making significant contributions to science, they were nearly equalled by Jesuits during the same period. Regardless of their specific and distinctive contributions, both Protestant and Catholic thinking in the sixteenth and seventeenth centuries played important roles in the scientific revolution in Europe; indeed, the subsequent development of modern science as we know

---

26 Alfred North Whitehead, *Science and the Modern World* (Cambridge: Cambridge University Press, 1926), 16, 19.

it owes a great deal to both the Protestant Reformation and the Catholic "counter-reformation."[27] In this light, several scholars strove to find something distinctive within Western Christendom so that credit for the rise of science could be shared more broadly across the Western Christian tradition. This is the view long advocated by the physicist and Benedictine priest Stanley Jaki, who argued in his 1974 Gifford Lectures that it was rational theism that necessarily gave rise to modern science, and that this was manifest most fully in the Christian West.[28] Jaki made a significant, and for some even audacious, claim when he wrote, "While biblical monotheism owed nothing to Greek science, that science could develop into a true science only within a monotheistic matrix, which happened to be biblical through the mediation of Christianity."[29] For Jaki, it was the Christian monotheistic tradition, especially as it developed in the West, which was absolutely essential for the rise of science.

This account of the religious contribution to the origins of natural science falls short of providing a comprehensive theory of the relationship between monotheism and the rise of science. In the first place, it defines science in such a way that can only explain the kind of scientific approach and results arising in Western Europe in the sixteenth and seventeenth centuries.[30] It also assumes that only Christian monotheism contributed significantly and positively to the rise of science.

---

27 Cf. Gary Deason, "Reformation Theology and the Mechanistic Conception of Nature," in *God and Nature: Historical Essays on the Encounter between Christianity and Science*, eds. David Lindberg and Ronald Numbers (Berkeley: University of California Press, 1986), 172.

28 Stanley Jaki, *The Road of Science and the Ways to God* (Chicago: University of Chicago Press, 1978), 34ff.

29 Jaki, *The Road of Science and the Ways to God*, 153.

30 Jaki's view has been criticised as claiming too much, for instance in Amos Funkenstein, *Theology and the Scientific Imagination from the Middle Ages to the Seventeenth Century* (Princeton NJ: Princeton University Press, 1986), 360ff.

Proponents of this view argue that "theological assumptions unique to Christianity explain why science was born only in Christian Europe," and that "Christian theology is essential for the rise of science."[31]

However, a cautionary note must be sounded here. As Noah Efron aptly observed, "One cannot recount the history of modern science without acknowledging the crucial importance of Christianity. However, this does not mean that Christianity and Christianity alone produced modern science."[32] When we look more foundationally at what science is, and the philosophical and methodological presuppositions which lay at its heart, the picture quickly becomes more complex.

## *Science arose due to the influence of Judaism and Talmudic discourse*

The oldest of the Abrahamic monotheistic faiths has made the fewest formal claims of responsibility for the rise of science.[33] However, many of the features of Christian and Islamic thought that may have aided the rise of science actually originated in Judaism. As Harold Turner points out, with reference to early Hebrew religion and its relation to science,

> The Hebrew conviction is that the world around us is made by this … good, rational and consistent creator. It therefore reflects its maker and so is itself morally, rationally, and consistently ordered. And we ourselves as creatures also

31 So, Rodney Stark, *For the Glory of God. How Monotheism Led to Reformations, Science, Witch Hunts and the End of Slavery* (Princeton NJ: Princeton University Press, 2004).

32 Noah Efron, "Myth 9: That Christianity Gave Birth to Modern Science," in Numbers, *Galileo Goes to Jail*, 82.

33 For a useful discussion of the relationship of science and Judaism, see Hava Tirosh-Samuelson, "Nature in the Sources of Judaism," in *Daedalus* (Fall 2001): 99–124. It is thought that the article was prompted in response to claims that Judaism, along with Christianity, is responsible for the modern ecological crisis. It gives a good overview of Judaism and its view of the natural world.

reflect our maker with minds that can work rationally and consistently and so be capable of understanding a universe structured in the same way. The related forms of order and coherence are prerequisites for science.[34]

The Talmud contains many references to the science of its day and links the knowledge of the natural world with the knowledge of God. For instance, in the Babylonian Talmud, we read of

> the one who knows how to calculate the cycles and planetary courses but does not know the Scripture. The Scripture says of such persons, "They do not regard the work of the Lord, neither have they considered his actions." (Shabbat, 75a)

The influence of Jewish philosophers, physicians, and scientists throughout medieval Christendom and early Islam, especially Moses Maimonides, must also be noted, as well as the significant number of Jewish scientists in recent centuries. It has been suggested that the Talmudic method of argumentation and the interaction with other faiths through the centuries of diaspora have contributed to an openness to critical thinking; this, in turn, played a key part in the development of scientific thought.[35] Certainly the influence of Jewish thought and culture played a role in the rise of science.

### Science began its rise in Islamic thought

Before the great strides within Western, post-Reformation Christendom, and even before the medieval rediscovery of Aristotle, a significant period of advancement in scientific thinking and discovery had occurred in the Islamic world.

It is undisputed that the early Islamic world borrowed

---

34 Harold Turner, *The Roots of Science. An Investigative Journey through the World's Religions* (Auckland: Deepsight Trust, 1998), 55.

35 There is an interesting analogous discussion of the impact of Talmudic discussion on the Jewish mind in explaining the great success in chess, at the highest levels, of so many Jewish players. See, for instance, David Spanier, *Total Chess* (New York: Dutton, 1984), 159ff.

heavily from preceding cultures for scientific, philosophical, and medical knowledge. The major source of this inherited knowledge was the Hellenistic culture and literature of the Greeks. However, did Islamic scholars and scientists simply pass on the knowledge of the Greeks? George Sarton, the eminent mid-twentieth century historian of science, put this view forward at the conclusion of his essay, "The End of Greek Science and Culture," when he wrote:

> Modern science is the continuation of fructification of Greek science and would not exist without it. .... Greek scholars were driven out of the Greek world and helped to develop Arabic science. Later the Arabic writing was translated into Latin ... and into our own vernaculars. The treasure of Greek science, most of it at least, came to us through that immense detour.[36]

However, Islamic science was far more than an "immense detour" from the Greeks to the medieval Christian West.

Muslim philosophers and scientists, such as Abū ʿAlī Ibn Sīnā (Avicena, d. 1037) and Alī Ibn al-Haytham (ʿAlhazen, 965–1039), were far more than simple forerunners of modern science in their methodologies and results. Centuries before science began to take significant hold in the Christian West, remarkable advances were being made by Muslim scholars. In philosophy, in addition to Ibn Sīnā (who was also a noted physician), al-Kindī, al-Fārābī, and Averroes stand out. The Persian Abu Bakr al Rāzī is remembered for his original contributions to medicine and for his collation of Indian, Greek, and Middle Eastern medical knowledge. Jābir Ibn Hayyān is remembered for what we would now call chemistry—though this science at the time coexisted with alchemy. In the field of astronomy and cosmology, Abū Maʿshar al-Balkhī, Al-Battani, Ibn Yunis, and ʿAbd al-Rahmān al-Sūfī were all well

---

36 George Sarton, *Ancient Science and Modern Civilization* (New York: Harper & Brothers, 1954), 111.

known. Furthermore, Ibn al-Haytham, or `Alhazen, was an accomplished mathematician, physicist, and astronomer. He was also a pioneer in the field of optics, demonstrating that Euclid and Ptolemy were wrong about the eye sending out rays of light to view objects but rather that it received rays of light from objects viewed. However, it was not only his technical abilities that caused him to stand out: he relentlessly examined and questioned existing theories, rejecting those that did not match the physical data. He articulated an inductive method, centuries before Bacon, and set out the steps for formulating and verifying hypotheses. The questions he asked about the natural world were intentional and systematic, and he anticipated many achievements of science in the West by at least six centuries, not only in the area of technical knowledge but also, more critically, in methodology.[37]

From the tenth to the thirteenth centuries, significant centres of scientific learning existed in the Islamic world from Cordova in Spain and Cairo in Egypt to Baghdad and Basra in the East; these centres were unparalleled up to that time.[38] In fact, most would readily agree with Jamil Ragep, a historian of science at the University of Oklahoma, who said, "Nothing in Europe could hold a candle to what was going on in the Islamic world until about 1600."[39]

------

37 Cf. Muhammad Saud, *The Scientific Method of Ibn al-Haytham* (Islamabad: Islamic Research Institute, 1990) and S. Nomanul Haq, "Moments in the Islamic Recasting of the Greek Legacy: Exploring the Question of Science and Theism," in T. Peters, M. Iqbal, and S. Haq, eds., *God, Life, and the Cosmos: Christian and Islamic Perspectives* (Aldershot, UK: Ashgate, 2002).

38 Cf. Stephen Mason, *A History of the Sciences* (New York: Macmillan, 1962), 95; Syed Nomanul Haq, "Moments in the Islamic Recasting of the Greek Legacy: Exploring the Question of Science and Theism," in T. Peters, M. Iqbal, and S. Haq, eds., *God, Life, and the Cosmos.*

39 Jamil Ragep, cited by Dennis Overbye, "How Islam Won, and Lost, the Lead in Science," *The New York Times*, October 30, 2001. The decline of science in the Islamic world is often blamed in part on the influence of Abu

## Science began with the Nestorian physicians and translators under the Abbasids

Islamic science, of course, did not arise out of a vacuum. Among the contributing factors to its golden era was the Nestorian Christian contribution to developments in medicine, science, and philosophy in and around Baghdad from 786 to 1258 CE. Le Coz even suggested that they are largely to be credited with the rise of science during this period.[40] Although Le Coz overstates his case, to the detriment of the outstanding Muslim contributions of this period, figures such as Hunyan ibn Ishaq, Ishaq ibn Hunayn, Uhanna Ibn Sarabiyum, Jibrail ibn Bukhtishu, and many other prominent Nestorian Christians certainly played a vital role.[41] The significance of Hunyan ibn Ishaq (808–873), the first and greatest of the translators of Greek philosophical texts, can hardly be overestimated. He threw himself into the massive task of translating Greek medical and philosophical texts into Arabic and Syriac and gathered around him a team composed mostly of fellow Nestorians, who had the advantage of a Greek language background. He

---

Hamid al-Ghazali. Cf. for example Hillel Ofek, "Why the Arabic World Turned Away from Science," in *The New Atlantis. A Journal of Technology and Society*, (Winter, 2011). However, al-Ghazali's influence was likely more complex than such assessments assume. As a theologian he was concerned about some of the influences of philosophy, but he also had many positive assessments (cf., for instance, Hassan Hassan, "Don't Blame It on al-Ghazali," *Qauntara.de*, 2103). This is a significant point, as some would like to argue that it was a theologian, writing as a theologian, who brought an end to the golden age of science in Islam rather than advancing it.

40 Cf. R. Le Coz, *Les médecins nestoriens au Moyen Âge: Les maîtres des Arabes* (Paris: L'Harmattan, 2004); and Syed Nomanul Haq, "Myth 4: That Medieval Islamic Culture Was Inhospitable to Science," in Numbers, *Galileo Goes to Jail*, 39 40.

41 For a more thorough discussion of the Nestorian contribution to the medicine and science of the Islamic golden age see the upcoming book by M. Worthing, *Nestorian Christian Contributions to Medicine and Science in the Golden Age of Islam under the Abbasid Caliphs of Baghdad 786–1258 CE*, forthcoming, Morning Star.

personally translated 116 separate works. His renown was such that he served as court physician to Caliph al-Mutwakkil for many years and was also the first head of the famous Baghdad library and translation centre, known as the House of Wisdom. Furthermore, Hunyan was far from alone. His great contemporary, the physician Jibrail ibn Bukhtishu (d. 870), stood at the head of a family dynasty of Nestorian Christian physicians and scholars that would span ten generations.[42] Jibrail ibn Bukhtishu authored several medical texts and had a profound influence on the emerging medical and scientific tradition in Baghdad.

Overall, the Nestorians played a vital part in the translation movement, especially the translation of medical texts. They were key contributors to the development of the Islamic hospital,[43] to original medical research with notable contributions to the anatomy of the eye, pharmacology, the description of trachomatous pannus, the description of the placebo effect, and the development of a system of categorisation of medicines according to their effect. They also played a significant role in establishing the practice of medicine as an ethical calling.

### The role of the Neoplatonists: Origen, Augustine, and the Cappadocians

Going back even further, there are contributions from the early Christian period that are often overlooked. The period was dominated by Platonic and Neoplatonic philosophy; the best Christian thinkers of the era were heavily influenced by this thinking and, in many cases, contributed to it.

---

42 The name "Bukhtishu" means "servants of Jesus" in Farsi, or perhaps the name is derived from an older form of Persian in which case the translation would be "one who is freed by Christ." See Husain Nagamia, "Pioneers of Islamic Medicine series no. 2: The Bukhtishus," (International Institute of Islamic Medicine), 7. In either case, it would have been eminently clear to their contemporaries that the Bukhtishus were followers of Yishu, that is, Jesus.
43 Peter Pormann and Emilie Savage-Smith, *Medieval Islamic Medicine* (Washington, DC: Georgetown University Press, 2007), 96–97.

Because Aristotelianism is generally viewed as the more fertile philosophical ground for the natural sciences, the contributions of those coming out of this period are often not taken into account. However, there was a Neoplatonic science, and Christian thinkers such as Origen, Augustine, and the Cappadocians made significant contributions to it. Origen, in fact, is credited with being one of the co-founders of Neoplatonism. Augustine was concerned not just about thinking about God but also about the world that God created. It was, in fact, Augustine's theological reflections that led him to produce what is considered the first essentially correct understanding of the nature of time. He left no doubt that as soon as there was matter, there was process and there was time. In *The City of God* Augustine wrote:

> For if eternity and time are rightly distinguished by this, that time does not exist without some movement and transition, while in eternity there is no change, who does not see that there could have been no time had not some creature been made, which by some motion could give birth to change—the various parts of which motion and change, as they cannot be simultaneous, succeed one another—and thus, in these shorter or longer intervals of duration, time would begin? … Then assuredly the world was made, not in time, but simultaneously with time.[44]

And the Cappadocians, the bedrock thinkers of the Eastern Christian tradition, integrated the best of the science of their day (which was essentially Neoplatonic) with their theological reflections on creation, the world around them, and human nature:

> Basil's *Hexaemeron* (the "Six Days" of Creation) both employs and critiques the philosophical cosmology of his day. His brother Gregory of Nyssa's *De hominis opificio*

---

44 Augustine, *The City of God*, trans. Marcus Dods (New York: Random House, 1950), XI. 6, 350.

(*On the Creation of the Human Being*) borrows elements of Platonic and Aristotelian anthropology, mixed with the medical theories of Galen, while nevertheless defining a uniquely Christian theological anthropology. … For these two brother bishops and theologians in fourth-century Cappadocia, there was no inherent conflict between science and their Christian faith. Gregory, in his *Life of Moses*, allegorized Moses' command to the Israelites to steal the gold of the Egyptians as an instruction for Christians to appropriate the scientific knowledge of Hellenistic culture.[45]

## Science began its rise with Greek philosophy and its turn toward monotheism

The Nestorians, whom we considered earlier, were especially significant because of the link that they provided to the scientific, medical, and philosophical knowledge of the Greeks. Indeed, it was the Greek philosophers who were vital for the foundational ideas that undergirded the progress of science in the golden age of Islam as well as in medieval Europe. Importantly, many of the strides that the Greeks made occurred at the very time they were moving intellectually away from the predominant polytheism of their culture and toward a philosophical monotheism. As Stephen Mason points out:

> Plato saw that any philosophy with a claim to generality must include a theory as to the nature of the universe. Such a theory could be subordinate to ethics, politics, and theology, and, if suitably framed, it could enhance their cogency. Plato accordingly evolved a natural philosophy that was harmonious with, and subordinate to, his political and theological views. … [And] Plato's God differed from the gods of the Bronze Age in that he did not order the universe by a process of organic procreation … but by

---

45 Valerie Karras, "Orthodoxy and Science in the Fourth Century," in *Science and the Eastern Orthodox Church*, eds. Daniel Buxhoeveden and Gayle Woloschak (Aldershott, UK: Ashgate, 2011), 32.

realizing an intellectual design. The most important feature of the ordering of the universe from chaos according to Plato, was the formulation of a rational design for the world by the Creator.[46]

The writings of the Greeks, especially those of Aristotle, played a pivotal role in the golden era of Islamic philosophy, in the rise of universities in thirteenth-century Europe, and in the subsequent progress toward the scientific revolutions of the sixteenth and seventeenth centuries. We tend to partition these achievements from later scientific advances, but they were necessary preconditions for what followed. As Arieti and Wilson have indicated in their survey of the relationship between science and religion, the ancient Greeks, especially Plato and Aristotle, quickly realised the implications of scientific discoveries for religious faith.[47] While Aristotle's belief in a first cause, or prime mover, was not one of religious devotion, the intellectual movement toward belief in a single deity (though not necessarily in a creator of all things) was more than an incidental component of his worldview.

While the work of Aristotle has been foundational for advances in science in both Islam and medieval Christianity, an offshoot of Platonic thought, namely Neoplatonism, played an often-overlooked role. Georgio de Santillana calls Neoplatonism the most significant of "scientific religions" because it "provided the foundations for Christian philosophy."[48] Plotinus emphasised that there must be a source of all good, of all thought, of all being. This deity was so far removed from us that we can only describe what it is not: the so-called *via negativa*, which influenced early medieval

---

46 Stephen Mason, *A History of the Sciences* (New York: Macmillan, 1962), 37.

47 James Arieti and Patrick Wilson, *The Scientific and the Divine: Conflict from Ancient Greece to the Present* (Oxford: Rowman and Littlefield, 2003).

48 Giorgio de Santillana, *The Origin of Scientific Thought from Anaximander to Proclus, 600BC–500AD* (Chicago: University of Chicago Press, 1961), 306.

Christian thinking about God. Plotinus and his followers, including many Christian philosophers, held to a mystical view of reality in which the highest level of "substance" below the one God was the realm of Intellect, followed by the realm of Soul (which included metaphysical motion) and, below that, physical life and reality. While physical reality was not high on the hierarchy of substances (*hypostases*) relating to the one God, it was, significantly, part of the hierarchy of realities. Admittedly, the Neoplatonists did not make great advances in the natural sciences but neither was their contribution trivial. The great Christian thinkers in this tradition, Origen of Alexandria and Augustine of Hippo, as already noted, made their own contributions to the advancement of knowledge, including of the physical world. In Christian Neoplatonism, it is not so much the seeds of science that were preserved and passed on but the seeds "of future scientific imagination."[49]

## The historical nexus between monotheistic communities and the rise of science

The various parochial theories about religion and the rise of science that we have surveyed carry weight, in part, because the key periods of advancement in science tend to coincide with various strong monotheistic intellectual traditions. The advances of science in ancient Greece correspond with the emerging philosophical monotheism at the time of Plato and Aristotle. Scientific advances in the early Christian classical world correspond with the theological contributions of thinkers such as Origen of Alexandria and Augustine of Hippo. Scientific progress, especially in medicine, associated with the

---

49 De Santillana, *The Origin of Scientific Thought*, 312. De Santillana writes: "'What do I want to know?' St Augustine asks …. 'Nothing but God and the soul.' … But within the confines thus set, there arises the need for *a* science, the science of the soul: and thus Neoplatonism becomes the great philosophy and the chief science of the high Middle Ages; it stands under the invocation of Plato, while Aristotle comes in only later" (p. 312).

golden era of Islam in and around Baghdad under the Abbasids, corresponds with the prevalent Muslim intellectual culture of that era and the strong Nestorian Christian community. Many advancements in the late medieval and early Renaissance period of Europe owe much to the thought of thinkers like Thomas Aquinas. Advancements made in seventeenth-century Catholic lands were strongly linked to the Jesuits. And the explosion of scientific advances in seventeenth and eighteenth-century Europe, particularly England, coincided with the pervasive influence of various forms of Protestantism.

There is no shortage, historically, of correlations that have been put forward linking strong monotheistic intellectual traditions and eras of significant scientific advancement. However, does a correlation of monotheistic environments with periods of growth in science equate to a cause-effect relationship?[50] Furthermore, if such a relationship exists, can it be assumed that monotheism is the only or even the primary causative factor? The fact that these assumptions are often made uncritically has opened the door for a number of objections to be raised against the idea that monotheism played a positive role in the rise of science. Before we take a fresh look at the basic thesis that monotheism played a decisive role in the rise of science, and the philosophical arguments that support this thesis, these objections must be addressed.

---

50 This is the objection raised, for instance, by Richard Carrier, among others. Cf. "Christianity Was Not Responsible for Modern Science," 399.

## PART TWO

# Objections to the proposition that monotheism played a key role in the development of science

## *Objection 1: Competing theories cancel one another out*

The fact that significant strides toward modern science were made in various contexts associated with monotheistic worldviews has countered overly confident claims that the rise of science is solely linked to a single monotheistic tradition. In fact, it could be argued that the various theories concerning the rise of science and their links to specific monotheistic traditions actually cancel one another out.[1] The proponents of the arguments for science arising specifically out of a single monotheistic context must necessarily argue against the claims of competing religious traditions in making their case. This is most often achieved by defining science in such a way that it corresponds to advances associated with one particular era, to the exclusion of all others.

Those suggesting that modern science arose out of some form of Protestant thought tend to argue that the forms of science prior to the Protestant Reformation did not meet key requirements to qualify as science in the fullest sense. At the same time, contemporary advances arising out of Roman Catholic or competing Protestant circles are often downplayed or ignored. The upshot of the multiplicity of such openly parochial arguments is that each one devotes much effort to countering the claims of rival religious traditions. Thus, the end result is that the various proponents of a strong link between the rise of science and some particular form of monotheistic

---

1 See, for instance, Jerry Coyne, "Did Christianity (and Other Religions) Promote the Rise of Science?," who writes: "If you think of science as rational and empirical investigation of the natural world, it originated not with Christianity but with the ancient Greeks, and was also promulgated for a while by Islam."

belief have often done much work to void one another's claims.

The case for a strong link between the rise of science and monotheism is not, however, thereby disproved. A cluster of competing claims, each of which seeks to make its own case by discrediting its rivals, operate on the assumption that only one claim can have ultimate merit. Such a diffuse and parochial approach does not consider the possibility that all have valid claims or that we must look to some factor(s) that they share in common to explain their contribution to the rise of science.

### Objection 2: *Scientific strides were also made in non-monotheistic cultures*

We are continually upgrading our assessment of the technical achievements and abilities of ancient societies. The early Greeks, Persians, Babylonians, Indians, Incas, and Chinese, to name some of the more prominent, were capable of great feats of building and engineering which required advanced understanding of mathematics, geometry, metal working, etc. Glass was formed, mirrors produced, and (in some cases) electricity even appears to have been known. Remarkably accurate observations of the stars were made (often for purposes of astrology), and a knowledge of medicine and anatomy were available that were not equalled again for many centuries. As Coyne states the objection, "Geometry was invented by polytheists (ancient Greeks); do we give polytheism credit for geometry, then?"[2]

If all these things had been achieved in cultures that were not monotheistic, can it be argued that monotheism contributed anything essential to the rise of science? Or, as Coyne suggests, should polytheism be credited with the achievements made in earlier eras?

It is crucial for the argument being made about monotheism

---

2 Jerry Coyne, "Did Christianity (and other religions) promote the rise of science?"

and science, and for understanding the history of science, to distinguish between science and technology. The two are closely connected. Advances in scientific understanding are generally followed by advances in technology and sometimes vice versa. However, the two are not identical. Most historians of science make a distinction between the technological knowledge and ability exhibited in ancient civilisations and what developed later, referring to the former as precursors to modern science or simply as ancient science.[3] The understanding of maths and geometry are impressive achievements in many ancient civilisations and other early cultures. We find, for instance, the skills needed to predict an eclipse of the sun or the basic knowledge of practical physics required for many ancient war machines. But the generally held view is that these things alone are not considered to qualify as science in the modern sense. We fail to find these either because they were not present, or they were not recorded, or in some other way passed down. We do not have any clear evidence from these societies of the quest for understanding why things work the way they do and how the knowledge of these various workings are interconnected, or of an articulated methodology for expanding our understanding of the natural world. To some extent, these kinds of questions must have been present, and this must be acknowledged. But the consistent and documented pursuit of an integrated

---

3 Cf., for instance, Stephen Mason, *A History of the Sciences*, 12–15. Also, Walter Libby, in his classic work *An Introduction to the History of Science* (Boston: Houghton Mifflin Company, 1917) highlighted the practical nature of ancient sciences, called ancient medicine "the foster-mother of many sciences," and reminds us of how different ancient science and medicine were to what later evolved in the example of Babylonian physicians; Babylonian physicians received by law a large sum if their surgery was successful, but if the patient died or lost their sight, etc., then the physician was to have his hands cut off so he could practise the art no more (p. 12). While much practical knowledge was obtained that proved necessary to the later growth of science, there is a stark contrast in approach between the knowledge of ancient civilisations and what began to emerge in the later period of classical Greek civilisation.

understanding the natural world (i.e., science as we know it) is something first found clearly among the ancient Greeks.

### Objection 3: Different forms of monotheism challenge the claim that monotheism is a common factor

It can be argued that the differences in the forms of monotheism among Judaism, Christianity, and Islam suggest there is no common link in the influence they may have contributed toward the rise of science. It is well known that the three traditions have, sometimes even within themselves, distinct ways of understanding how God works in the world, from forms of atomism to the ideas of process theology. Furthermore, Jewish and Muslim scholars have long asked just how monotheistic Christian belief actually is, given its commitment to the doctrine of the Trinity.

The implications for our understanding of the natural world are remarkably similar in all forms of monotheism; this is regardless of whether God acts through natural causes only, in what some describe as a non-interventionist model, or whether every single action and movement of every molecule is determined by God. The belief in a divine rationality that creates a comprehensible and rational world is present in each case. Also present is the quest for understanding the physical processes of the world. Those who have been much more radically deterministic in their understanding, whether Muslim atomists or Calvinist Puritans, do not appear to have held back from asking questions of nature because of their belief that God determines each action and process.[4] In every case, the physical world is seen as distinct from God, who

---

4 Coyne, however, assumes this would have been the case. He argues that "all progress in science, whether ancient or modern, came from ignoring or rejecting the idea of divine intervention. Even if theories were inspired by thoughts of God, they were substantiated or disproven by tacitly assuming a godless universe—that is, by employing methodological naturalism." Coyne, "Did Christianity (and other religions) promote the rise of science?"

created the world to behave in a regular and patterned manner, accessible to our understanding. As much as we might like to think that our own particular version of monotheism gives some unique advantage to the scientific endeavour, the truth appears to be that the influence may be from monotheism more generally. Whatever it is about monotheism that may have played a critical role in the rise of science, it is common to the basic idea of a single creator God and is not dependent upon any particular expression of monotheistic belief.

## Objection 4: Monotheistic religion opposed the advance of science

The claims of religious opposition to science made by Draper and White are generally held by historians of science to be exaggerated and, in some cases, even manufactured. However, it cannot be denied that there were incidents of opposition to the sciences and to individual scientists, often carried out on "religious grounds." Within the Western Christian tradition, two sad examples include the burning at the stake of the Spanish physician and contributor to the understanding of the circulatory system, Michael Servetus, on the orders of John Calvin at Geneva on 27 October 1553, and of Giordano Bruno, monk and astronomer, in Rome on 17 February 1600. While accusations of heretical religious views played key roles in both tragic executions, the fact cannot be overlooked that each was also a significant scientific thinker of their time.

Jerry Coyne, author of *Why Evolution is True*, posted eleven reasons on his website of the same name as to why the idea that science came from religion must be rejected. His fifth reason is this:

> Religion has of course also repressed the search for knowledge. Not only do we have the cases of Galileo and Bruno, but also the active discouragement of the use of reason by many church fathers, especially Martin Luther,

who made statements like this: "Reason is a whore, the greatest enemy that faith has; it never comes to the aid of spiritual things, but more frequently than not struggles against the divine Word, treating with contempt all that emanates from God." And freethinkers like Spinoza were regularly persecuted by religion (Judaism in his case).[5]

As already pointed out, the very real persecution of Bruno was based on his theology, not his science, and the difficulties (much less severe!) experienced by Galileo had much to do with his personal conflict with the pope. Coyne's argument about Luther is surprising, as Luther's support for the natural sciences and their independence from theology is well documented.[6] The context in which Luther is quoted here, in the colourful language he sometimes employed, was about reason as it was used by medieval scholastic theology to interpret the Bible and theological truths. He was criticising theological scholasticism and making no reference to ordinary human logic or reason, especially not as it might be employed in understanding the physical world. To take Luther's use of reason in this context and apply it to reason as we understand it in the sciences is the fallacy of false equivalence, that is, of suggesting that one thing (Luther's critique of scholastic "reason") is actually another (a critique of "reason" as applied to examining the natural world). It is a stretch, at best, to make a serious claim that religion, in this case Christianity, made an orchestrated and sustained effort to "repress the search for knowledge."

This is, of course, not to say that some religious teachers and leaders did not indeed fear science and oppose its findings. It is not surprising that some religious leaders, as they saw the rising influence of science, sought either to stop or control science.

---

5 Jerry Coyne, "Did Christianity (and Other Religions) Promote the Rise of Science?"

6 Cf., for instance, M. Worthing, "Luther on the Border of Superstition and Science," in *Martin Luther: A Wild Boar in the Lord's Vineyard*, 141ff.

Similarly, some modern scientists seem to have an aversion to religion. However, this does not imply that scientists in general or science as an entity is anti-religious. These incidents, regardless of their exact circumstances, do not negate the role played by monotheistic belief as a whole in the rise of science. Rather, they more strongly represent a political reaction to a perceived, and at times real, loss of influence and power. Despite the responses and actions of some religious officials, it would seem, as Harold Nebelsick put it, that "the main motivating force behind the pursuit of natural knowledge from the time of Babylon and Greece in the East to the time of the Renaissance in the West was theological rather than scientific."[7]

## Objection 5: Not all monotheistic cultures show evidence of interest in scientific thought

If there was something particular about monotheistic religion and thought that provided a fertile ground for the rise of science, then why did so many monotheistic cultures show little or no trace of such developments? Why did little happen within Christianity until the thirteenth century, and then largely only in the West? Why did more development not continue to occur among some of the Muslim societies that made such impressive early strides? Or why, in the long history of Judaism before the rise of Christian and Islamic monotheism, did nothing like modern science begin to break through?[8]

Richard Carrier argued that Christianity's claim to have given rise to science,

---

7 Harold Nebelsick, *Circles of God: Theology and Science from the Greeks to Copernicus* (Edinburgh: Scottish Academic Press, 1985), xiii.

8 It should be noted, however, that Jewish thinkers played important roles in the key periods of the development of modern science. At the height of the golden era of Muslim science Maimonides was a famed philosopher and medical expert who went from Muslim Spain to serve as personal physician to Saladin. Jewish philosophers and scientists also played a role in the explosion of scientific thinking that began to occur in Europe from the seventeenth century. Judaism, even in diaspora, played its role in the rise of science.

violates one of the most basic principles of causality: when the cause is in place, its effect is seen. Christianity fully dominated the whole of the Western world from the fifth to the fifteenth century, and yet in all those thousand years there was no Scientific Revolution ... [and] no Scientific Revolution in the Eastern half of the Christian world either, which had none of the West's excuses. The East was not overrun by barbarians and remained prosperous and developed for five centuries.[9]

One response to this lack of progress in science during this period is to point out that the existence of a strong monotheistic worldview, however instrumental, is not sufficient in itself to explain the rise of modern science in its various phases. It is not simply Christianity, but other factors as well that appear to have been important, working in combination. Carrier assumes that the argument is that Christianity and Christianity alone provided the fertile soil for modern science. Unfortunately, some of the recent advocates of this view seem to argue just this. However, the argument for monotheism in general, and Christianity in particular, having such a role is much more nuanced. Other factors must also be considered. Political stability, intellectual freedom, relative economic prosperity, a culture of learning, and even the invention of the printing press have all been vital factors. As Whitehead put it nearly a century ago:

> It is unnecessary to tell in detail the various incidents which marked the rise of science: the growth of wealth and leisure; the expansion of the universities; the invention of printing; the taking of Constantinople; Copernicus; Vasco da Gama; Columbus; the telescope. The soil, the climate, the seeds, were there, and the forest grew.[10]

---

9 Richard Carrier, "Christianity Was Not Responsible for Modern Science," in *The Christian Delusion. Why Faith Fails*, ed. John Loftus (Amherst, NY: Prometheus Books, 2010), 397.
10 Whitehead, *Science and the Modern World*, 20.

It could also be argued that there were deficiencies of monotheistic understanding and practice in those regions and eras in which science did not thrive that explain the lack of progress in scientific thinking. In other words, Carrier's claim that Christianity "fully dominated" the Western world from 500 to 1500 CE is misleading. The church as an institution, and often a corrupt institution at that, certainly had a dominant influence during this period. However, many other non- and sub-Christian ideologies and structures were also present. The feudal structure, pagan superstitions, the knightly concept of chivalry, the mass migrations of peoples, and other factors all significantly influenced medieval life and thought, and not always in a positive way. However, none of these can be attributed to Christianity as a system of belief. Healthy and properly understood monotheism appears to have gone hand-in-hand with tolerance and intellectual freedom. Where these were suppressed (or were not able to develop), the positive aspects of monotheism that encouraged scientific investigation of the physical world were also unable to flourish.

The fact that the mere presence of monotheistic belief did not always lead toward further steps along the road to modern science does not necessarily mean that vital contributions were not made by such belief systems.

## Part Three

# The case for monotheism as a significant contributing cause in the rise of science

We have seen that numerous studies exist that demonstrate a link between various phases in the rise of science and specific monotheistic traditions. We have also looked at the major objections to the thesis that monotheism played a decisive role in the rise of science. While valid points have been raised in these objections, none of them have been able to dismiss the theory. However, if monotheistic belief played a vital role in the rise of science, more is needed to make this case. There must also be a positive explanation of the contributions of monotheism that helped produce fertile soil for the rise of science. However, before these arguments are put forward, we must clarify what is not being claimed, as well as what cannot be claimed.

## *What a theory of the role of monotheism in the rise of science cannot claim*

The case for the role of monotheism in the rise of science has been briefly reviewed in our survey of the arguments for the role played by individual monotheistic traditions. These various parochial arguments have tended to make three fundamental mistakes, which any case for the role of monotheism in the rise of science must avoid.

1. These arguments err in those instances in which they claim that one particular religion (Judaism, Christianity, or Islam) or one branch of a particular religion (Calvinism, English Puritanism, Protestantism) alone gave rise to science.

2. These arguments err when they assume that science arose substantially in a single era (associated with a specific religious tradition), while ignoring the reliance of the developments of this particular period on previous steps or stages in the rise of science.

3. These arguments err when the positive role of a particular religious context or contribution, once established, is treated as if it were the only cause for the rise of science. A contributing cause is not, *ipso facto*, a sufficient cause. The presence of other significant factors influencing progress in science in a particular era cannot be ignored.[1]

Any theory concerning the role played by monotheism in the rise of science must avoid these errors by not overstating its claims in the pursuit of making a case for a particular monotheistic tradition, or even monotheism generally, regardless how persuasive this case may appear. The following arguments, therefore, are (1) made regarding monotheism generally, (2) recognise that modern science progressed in stages through numerous distinct historical periods, and (3) acknowledge that influences apart from monotheism also played significant roles in the rise of science.

### *The explanatory value of monotheism for the rise of science*

Scientific method places much weight upon explanation. The more data a theory explains, the more weight that theory is given. If the monotheism-science theory is credible, then more is needed than a series of intriguing historical connections. The historical correlation of monotheistic belief systems and advances in science form a strong argument that monotheism,

---

1 As Noah Efron observed: "Even if you look no further than Europe during 'the Scientific Revolution' for the origins of science, religion is only part of what you will find. … Commerce has as much to do with the rise of modern science as Christianity did. … A great many other forces affected the growth of modern science in Europe. Some have found that the invention or importation of important technology, like clocks and especially the printing press, gave a boost to the sorts of inquiry that in time developed into modern science. Others have found that changes in European political organization spurred the development of science in complicated ways, and still others have found that … Europe's great legal systems influenced the development of both scientific theory and practice." Efron, "Myth 9: That Christianity Gave Birth to Modern Science," in Numbers, *Galileo Goes to Jail*, 85–86.

at the very least, did not hinder the growth of science. However, more than historical and geographic proximity of the two is needed to make the case that monotheistic belief systems have actually positively contributed to the rise of science. Amos Funkenstein put the problem bluntly when he wrote:

> That one can draw many meaningful connections between medieval theology and early modern science is certain. That without the former, the latter would never have emerged or advanced in any guise is neither demonstrable nor plausible.[2]

Correlation is not proof of a cause and effect relationship. Even if a cause and effect relationship could be established, it might be an unrelated or contributing factor rather than a necessary cause. The more important question, given the apparent correlation between monotheistic traditions and the growth of science, is this: what specific advantage or advantages did monotheism provide for the rise of science? If science flourished within monotheistic intellectual environments, what features of monotheism may reasonably be considered to have contributed to this? Furthermore, to what extent do these advantages help explain the rise of science in its various forms and phases from the time of the ancient Greeks through the golden era of Muslim philosophy and on to the explosion of scientific advances arising out of sixteenth and seventeenth-century Christian Europe?

The historical evidence that revolutions in scientific thinking arose in places and at times in which healthy forms of monotheism existed provides the basic observational data upon which a "hunch" is formed. This then gives rise to a theory concerning a possible cause–effect relationship between the two phenomena. The next step in theory formation is the demonstration that the theory has explanatory value. In other words, is it capable of explaining why things happened the way they did?

---

2 Funkenstein, *Theology and the Scientific Imagination*, 362.

The genius of Darwin's contribution to understanding natural evolution was not to be found in his observations of evolutionary change within life forms. This had already been well documented through observation and in the fossil record before he published *On The Origin of Species*. Nor was it in the explanation of the biological mechanism by which changes could occur within organisms; this would occur only seven years after Darwin's landmark book, when the Augustinian monk Gregor Mendel published his study on the genetic mutation of peas.[3] The genius of Darwin's contribution was his explanation of how and why these changes remain within species and why they seem to provide an evolutionary direction, namely, the process of natural selection through the survival of the fittest.

If we are to consider a theory about how monotheistic thought positively contributed to the growth of science, we must move beyond the correlation of periods of scientific revolution with that of monotheistic communities. We must examine what features, common to monotheistic belief systems, may have been significant factors in the rise of science and why these factors would have had such an influence.

## Monotheism created a context in which questions could be asked of the natural world

In the ancient world—that is to say, in the world as it was before the proclamation of Christ brought the God of Abraham, Isaac, and Jacob to the wider attention of the nations—there was little concept of secularity. Even among the Greeks, who gave us the antecedents for many of our modern philosophical systems through Plato and Aristotle, and spawned concepts such as democracy and the city-state, there was no room for the purely

---

3 Gregor Mendel, "Versuche über Pflanzenhybriden," in *Verhandlungen des naturforschenden Vereines in Brünn* 4 (1866):1–47. Regrettably, little attention was paid to this paper initially and Darwin was never aware of this key piece of the puzzle to which he had devoted his life.

secular. In the ancient religious centre of Delphi, for instance, one notes that the various treasure houses were all dedicated to the gods, and the Oracle of Delphi sat along the main way just beneath the Temple of Apollo. The city amphitheatre stood across from the temple, and its plays were dedicated to the exposition of the activities of the gods and their importance for our lives; this was often the case in other cities as well. Even the athletic field above the city was lined with religious monuments and its sporting events and sporting heroes dedicated to the gods. In Delphi, as in ancient cities and ancient thought in general, everything had its religious significance. In earlier, so-called primitive civilisations, individual trees, rocks, and hills all had their own spirits or gods.

What the ancient Jewish faith sought to accomplish in its own districts,[4] Christianity made a reality in much of the Mediterranean world. Later, Islam carried these ideas even further through the Middle East and beyond. The gods, spirits, and magic were taken out of rocks, trees, and hills. The high places were torn down or simply forgotten, and sacrality and divine power were concentrated in the one true God. Animism (the worship of spirits and ancestors within rocks and trees and other objects) and polytheism (the worship of multiple gods) were largely abandoned in favour of the worship of a single, all-powerful God.[5] The former high places, temples, altars, ceremonies, and sacred objects lost their power and sway over the masses. As sacrality became centralised in the being of God, particularly the Judeo-Christian God, the physical world itself became secularised. For the first time outside of Israel, one could truly distinguish between the sacred and the secular.

4 For a discussion of the impact of Hebrew monotheism on the process of desacralisation see Harold Turner, *The Roots of Science. An Investigative Journey Through the World's Religions* (Auckland: Deepsight Trust, 1998), 54ff.; and Max Weber, *Ancient Judaism* (New York: Free Press, 1952).
5 For further discussion of this process see Hans Schwarz, *The Search for God: Christianity - Atheism - Secularism - World Religions* (Minneapolis: Augsburg, 1975), 17ff.

An emerging natural science was no longer faced with the daunting task of challenging a sacred world filled with spirits, gods, holy places, and holy people. Monotheism, by its very nature, encouraged the asking of questions about the functions of the natural world. For this reason, Max Weber argued that this desacralisation of the world laid the groundwork for a scientific approach to the world.[6]

Why would this be the case? One might think that monotheism, especially those forms with strong affirmations of God's sovereignty, would have been little different to polytheism in the tendency to attribute all causes directly to the actions of a single deity; this would also eliminate the need to ask questions about natural causes. If a flood or drought occurred, then the questions to be asked would be: why was God angry, and what must we do to appease God? One might think that monotheism would simply have rolled up the functions of the various competing deities into one package. However, this is not what happened. Belief in one God led people to look increasingly to natural causes. H. Richard Niebuhr, in his extended essay, *Radical Monotheism and Western Culture*, argued that by its nature, "radical monotheism would include … reverence for beings, inorganic perhaps, perhaps ideal, that though not living claim the wondering and not exploitative attention of us other creatures that have the will-to-live." This is the case, explained Niebuhr, because "radical monotheism dethrones all absolutes short of the principle of being itself. At the same time, it reverences every relative existent."[7] This is because genuine monotheism calls us to value and be concerned with all things that come from the hand of the one God, including that which is not sentient and even that which is not animate.

---

6 Max Weber, *Gesammelte Aufsätze zur Religionssoziologie*, I, (Severus, 2015), 513.
7 H. Richard Niebuhr, *Radical Monotheism and Western Culture: With Supplementary Essays* (New York: Harper and Brothers, 1960), 37.

Additionally, it was commonly believed that a single, all-powerful God would create and govern the natural world in such a way as to follow regular and, therefore, comprehensible patterns. If nature is not itself divine but is the creation of the Divine One, then we can ask questions of nature or even conduct experiments on it. In this regard, monotheism provides a context in which science was free to evolve.

## Monotheism and the unity of knowledge

The second major contribution of monotheistic thought that must be considered is its emphasis on the unity of knowledge. The Muslim doctrine of *tawhid* is well-known. The unity of God has implications for the unity of what God creates and for the unicity of knowledge of the created world. It was commitment to the doctrine of *tawhid* that motivated many of the early Muslim philosophers. Christian thinkers likewise saw the correlation between the oneness of God (albeit understood in Trinitarian form) and the unity of knowledge about the world created by God.

If a single divine being is responsible for the whole of the created, natural order, then all knowledge about the natural world must be fundamentally interconnected. Monotheistic thinkers not only tended to ask after natural causes and explanations, but also to view these causes as fundamentally linked—having a common ground in the one creator God. As Wolfhart Pannenberg said,

> If God is sovereign as the Almighty Creator of everything, there should be no animal, no human being, and certainly not human nature, there should be no stone on this earth that could be adequately understood without this God. In other words, we don't need some prior decision of faith, we only need to remove our prejudices and look on reality as it presents itself.[8]

---

8 Wolfhart Pannenberg, "Theta Phi Discussion with Wolfhart Pannenberg," *The Asbury Theological Journal* 4:2 (Fall 1991), 24–25.

Monotheism not only set people free to ask the questions of nature necessary for the emergence of science, but it also suggested a unitary view of the world and the knowledge of the world that has proved vital for the rise of science—from the Greek philosophers, to the golden era of Muslim philosophy and science, to the revolutions in scientific thinking in Western Europe. In other words, things happen in the natural world apart from the whims of individual deities, and the explanations of these occurrences should not be viewed as unconnected.

### *The mind of God and the natural order*

Einstein once famously quipped that he was not interested in individual phenomena. "I want," he said, "to know the thoughts of God. The rest are mere details."[9] While it is inappropriate to take this comment as some sort of statement of faith on Einstein's part, it does illustrate the commonly held assumption among scientific thinkers that there is an underlying and unifying logic to the universe. In this light, we can understand why one of the core assumptions of monotheism, that is, that a logical mind will produce a logical world, was important for the emergence of science. If the mind of God is coherent and comprehensible, then the world which God creates will also be coherent and comprehensible; thus, it can be approached and investigated with the expectation that it can be understood. The tendency to ask questions of the natural world was not only a result of the freedom that monotheism provided to ask such questions, but it also arose from the belief in divine intelligence. Alfred North Whitehead saw belief in divine rationality, especially as it arose in Western conceptions of God, as vital for the rise of science in Europe. Whitehead believed that the formation of the scientific movement in Europe was only possible because of the belief that "every detailed occurrence can be correlated with its antecedents in a perfectly definite manner." However,

---

9 Cited in Walter Isaacson, *Einstein: His Life and Universe* (New York: Simon & Schuster, 2007) and numerous other sources.

where did this belief come from? Whitehead argues:

> It must come from the medieval insistence on the rationality
> of God, conceived as with the personal energy of Jehovah
> and with the rationality of a Greek philosopher. Every detail
> was supervised and ordered: the search into nature could
> only result in the vindication of the faith in rationality.[10]

In other words, if God is rational then there should
be an inherent intelligibility in the universe. Stanley Jaki
expressed this in relation to the Christian tradition. He said
that the Christian theism of the middle ages "manifested
a broadly shared conviction that a personal, rational, and
provident Being, absolute and eternal, is the ultimate source of
intelligibility insofar as he is the Creator of all things visible and
invisible."[11] It is this assumption concerning divine rationality
that underlies the well-known statement by Sir Isaac Newton:

> Since every particle of space is *always*, and every indivisible
> moment of duration is *every where*, certainly the Maker and
> Lord of all things cannot be *never* and *no where* … God is
> the same God, always and every where. He is omnipresent
> not *virtually* only, but also *substantially*; for virtue cannot
> subsist without substance. … It is allowed by all that the
> Supreme God exists necessarily; and by the same necessity
> he exists *always* and *every where*. … And thus much
> concerning God; to discourse of whom from the appearance
> of things, does certainly belong to Natural Philosophy.[12]

As historian of science John Hedley Brooke pointed out,
concerning the age in which Newton worked, the seventeenth-
century quest after the laws of nature can also be seen as a
quest to uncover the divine legislation that lies behind nature's
regularities.[13]

---

10 Whitehead, *Science and the Modern World*, 15–16.
11 Jaki, *The Road of Science and the Ways to God*, 34.
12 Isaac Newton, *Principia: The Mathematical Principles of Natural Philosophy* (New York: Daniel Adee, 1846), 505–6.
13 John Hedley Brooke, *Science and Religion: Some Historical Perspectives*

## *Monotheism and intellectual freedom*

Though examples of the suppression of intellectual freedom among the monotheistic traditions are sadly numerous, the source documents of Abrahamic monotheism, as well as the fundamental assumptions of philosophical monotheism, lead in an entirely different direction. A God whose existence and power does not depend upon our devotion, and who does not require our defense, is a God who can be questioned (Job, in the Book of Job, chapters 23–29) and who can respond to doubt with evidence rather than threat (Thomas, in the Gospel of John, 20:24–29). One of the unusual features of the monotheism characteristic of the Abrahamic faiths is that God can be questioned and even argued with. These stories are so well known that those who have grown up with them often take them for granted. However, Abraham negotiating with God over the fate of Sodom and Gomorrah, Job's questioning of God's actions toward him, the complaints of many of the prophets, Thomas's open expression of doubt when he hears the account of the resurrection appearance of Jesus—these are all quite remarkable in the context of the history of religious thought. Taken together, they have helped to foster and reinforce the idea that hard questions can be asked about God and the world.

A healthy monotheism produces sufficient confidence in its adherents to be able to live with religious and intellectual diversity. Human nature has often suppressed this tendency within monotheism, but when it has been rightly grasped (e.g., in the golden age of Islam under the Abbasids) the impact on the advance of scientific thinking has been profound.

## *Monotheism, peoples of the book, and literacy*

Numerous studies have been done on the impact of the reliance of Jews, Christians, and Muslims upon their sacred texts. It

(Cambridge: Cambridge University Press, 1991).

54

is not without significance that all three major monotheistic traditions are "religions of the book." While sacred texts were known to exist in other religious traditions, the role of written revelation in Judaism, Christianity, and Islam is unprecedented. The religious texts of these monotheistic religions served as a great impetus for literacy within their communities. Even as recently as Martin Luther's translation of the Bible into German, the availability of religious texts meant to be read by all has had immeasurable impact on literacy rates across the communities who have had these texts among them.

In earlier centuries, the existence of scribes and literate audiences able to read the sacred books that were copied out meant that other ideas could also be more readily written down. These could be exchanged between cultures and passed down through the generations. Monotheistic religions provided the language for treating complex topics in both metaphysical and natural philosophy, as well as an audience capable of understanding this language.

In his conclusion to *The Bible, Protestantism, and the Rise of Natural Science*, Peter Harrison argues that it was "the modern approach to texts, driven by the agenda of the reformers and disseminated through Protestant religious practices, [that] created the conditions which made possible the emergence of modern science."[14] While the approach to texts that Harrison outlines developed out of a particular period of Christian history, this could not have occurred without the existence of the texts themselves and the role they played within the community of faith.

## *The positive contribution of science to the advancement of monotheism*

We cannot discuss the interaction between monotheism and science as if the influence was always and only in one

14 Peter Harrison, *The Bible, Protestantism, and the Rise of Natural Science*, 266.

direction. In fact, indications of a positive influence of science upon the advancement of monotheism ultimately strengthens the argument that monotheism promoted the growth of science, as it further establishes the existence of a mutually beneficial relationship between the two. The fact that, in most instances (with the probable exception of the classical era of Greek philosophy), monotheistic thought systems historically preceded the scientific developments with which they are linked means that the focus has been put on the likely positive impact of monotheism on science. However, a case for progress in scientific thinking having a positive—and to some extent causative—effect on the development of monotheism could also be made, though it is a more complex argument.

In the case of Greek philosophical monotheism, it could be argued that the asking of questions of the natural world caused a movement away from the dominant polytheism of Greek culture and toward philosophical monotheism. The rise of Greek philosophical monotheistic thought, in turn, played a considerable and demonstrable role in easing the way for the acceptance of Christian monotheistic religion within late antiquity. Monotheism was long established in Hebrew thought but fought a long battle among the Israelites for ultimate acceptance. The kind of questions the ancient Hebrews asked of the world around them, as for instance in Job 38–39, may well indicate that the interest in finding explanations for the natural order of things existed at least alongside their commitment to monotheism. If monotheism and natural science "grew up" together and shared many of the same critical, individual thinkers, it is not unreasonable to assume that the natural sciences produced a context just as conducive to the continued growth and advancement of monotheism as vice versa.

Ultimately, an argument for science playing a critical role in giving rise to monotheism would need to rely on some form of reverse causality, or perhaps self-causality. In other words, the drive to ask questions of, and understand the workings of, the natural world was so strong that it somehow helped give rise to religious systems that were conducive to precisely this enterprise. Such phenomena are not unheard of in biological evolution, and there is no reason to exclude it from the evolution of ideas. If the desire to understand the physical world was stronger than the need to have deities responsible for every person, place, and event, then perhaps this need or desire played a role in bringing monotheism to the fore, which in turn played a decisive role in the "inevitable" emergence of natural science.

At the very least, the relationship between monotheistic belief and natural science is far more complex than we often imagine. Monotheistic traditions, however, should not fear the exploration of this link, as it would serve to confirm the historical congruence of monotheistic and scientific thought. Indeed, it would threaten only those adherents of monotheistic religion who have such a deficiency of humility as to assume that their religion must be the source of other positive intellectual systems and ideas but are themselves the beneficiaries of none of these.

## PART FOUR

The distinctive contribution of Christian monotheism

While monotheism, broadly understood, appears to have provided the fertile ground upon which modern science and the research culture associated with it could arise and flourish, individual monotheistic traditions certainly also made their own unique contributions. I will restrict my comments here to my own Christian tradition. There are features of Christian monotheism, it could be argued, which enhanced the support of the growth of science within those minds influenced by this faith tradition. The unique contributions of Christianity, however, must be understood as being built upon the foundation of the contribution of monotheism as a whole to the rise of science.

## The Trinity

Perhaps the obvious place to begin is also the most challenging: the Christian doctrine of the Trinity, which is the chief feature distinguishing Christian monotheism from Jewish and Islamic monotheism. There have been examples historically of scientists motivated by Christian thought to incorporate the doctrine of the Trinity in their conception of the natural world. Perhaps most notably among these is Johannes Kepler's unsuccessful attempt to conceive of the heavens in Trinitarian fashion.[1] However, it is the more subtle influences of Trinitarian

---

1 Kepler wrote, for instance, that "in the sphere … there are three regions, symbols of the three persons of the Holy Trinity—the centre, a symbol of the Father; the surface, of the Son; and the intermediate space, of the Holy Ghost." And he used this assumption to attempt a calculation of the respective densities of the three regions of the cosmic sphere of space based on the assumption that each must be equal in density, after the model of the Trinitarian God who created them. Cf. M. Worthing, *God, Creation, and Contemporary Physics*, 14.

thinking that may well have had a more genuine and positive influence. The doctrine of the Trinity has shaped many aspects of Christian thinking not only about God, but also about human relationships and the natural world. Christian conceptions of time, relationships, and of the inherent dynamism of all things have all grown out of the understanding of the doctrine of the Trinity. And the understanding of the whole-part relationships and structures of interrelatedness in nature have rich parallels with theological discussions of the triune nature of God.[2]

Easier perhaps to grasp is the influence that the view of Jesus as the Christ has had on the way Christians view the natural world. In fact, it could be argued that two of the most important contributions to the rise of science that are specific to Christianity concern Christology, which necessarily stands at the centre of Christian belief.[3]

*Incarnation*

From Augustine to Aquinas, from the Nestorian Christians of Islamic Persia to medieval Christian philosophers, from Puritans to Jesuits, there has been a broad contribution to the rise of science across the Christian spectrum. Central to a specifically Christian contribution to the rise of science is the doctrine of the incarnation. The theology of the incarnation affirms both the value of the material world and our scientific knowledge of this world. Within the philosophical milieu of ancient Hellenism, the value of the physical world was often relegated to secondary importance or even seen as an evil in

---

2 For explorations into links between the Christian doctrine of the Trinity and the natural sciences see Samuel Powell, *Participating in God. Creation and Trinity* (Minneapolis: Fortress Press, 2003); and Graham Buxton, *The Trinity, Creation and Pastoral Ministry. Imagining the Perichoretic God* (Milton Keynes, UK: Paternoster, 2005).

3 For a fuller discussion, see M. Worthing, "Some Brief Reflections on Christology and the Natural Sciences," *Lutheran Theological Journal* 47, no. 1. (May 2013): 4–9.

comparison to the value and reality of the spiritual realm. The idea that God, as a pure spiritual being, would take on human flesh was not only scandalous but preposterous. Long battles were fought within early Christianity against attempts by various forms of Gnostic and docetic movements to reject the idea that God could or would take on human flesh. The central affirmation of the incarnation that prevailed was not only a victory for orthodox Christian belief, but it also served to underscore in the minds of Christians the value of the physical world. If God took on human flesh, then the physical world has inherent worth. The incarnation dignifies the physical. It makes the physical something worth valuing, worth redeeming, and worth understanding.

The incarnation is an affirmation of the value and knowability of the physical world—including human beings. Included in the Christian understanding of the incarnation is also the idea that God in Christ suffers. The cruciform shape of Christian belief predisposes Christian thinkers to value the importance of struggle and suffering in the world—ideas which came very much to the fore with Darwin's concept of natural selection.[4] The doctrine of the incarnation is foundational for a Christian theology of nature.[5] It is one of the key formative doctrines for the Christian view of the natural world.

---

4 Cf. the insightful discussion of "Darwin's Gift to Theology," in John Haught, *God After Darwin. A Theology of Evolution* (Boulder, CO: Westview Press, 2000), 45ff.

5 T. F. Torrance said, "there must be a close coordination between theological concepts and physical concepts: which is, after all, the inescapable implication of the Christian doctrines of creation and incarnation and the inseparable relation between logos and being which they establish. This being the case, an essential place must be found for so-called 'natural theology', if only out of recognition of the fact that the interaction of God with the world grounds our conceiving of him within the relation of God to the world and of the world to God." Torrance, *Reality and Scientific Theology* (Edinburgh: Scottish Academic Press, 1985), 36–37.

## *Resurrection*

The incarnation does not stand alone in its role of affirming the value of the physical. The resurrection of Jesus is the other core component of Christology that undergirds the high Christian estimation of the natural world. Like the doctrine of the incarnation, the doctrine of the bodily resurrection of Jesus was difficult for many who were influenced by Hellenistic worldviews to accept. Once again, it was a clear affirmation of the importance of the physical. In the context of the Greek world, death was seen to be an escape from the prison of the physical body, not an affirmation of its necessity. The resurrection of Jesus, together with the affirmation of the incarnation, meant that orthodox Christology affirmed—in the strongest possible terms—the value of the physical world.

The traditional Christian insistence on a bodily resurrection of Jesus, and the future resurrection of all those who are in Christ, was in sharp contrast to Hellenistic views in which only the spiritual has ultimate value. From that view, the physical world, including our physical bodies, is little more than an encumbrance to be overcome. By insisting that human beings are spirit and body, even in the heavenly kingdom, the physical world was embraced and affirmed.

Christology, especially as expressed in the doctrines of the incarnation and resurrection, forms a significant part of the theological foundation for the natural sciences as they developed in recent centuries within the Christian-influenced Western world. Without these doctrines, it is unlikely that modern science would have been embraced with the vigour that it was within the intellectual world of Christianity. Christian faith affirms not only belief in God as creator of all things but also belief in God taking on human flesh and Christ rising from the dead and taking on a resurrected body. Such a faith should fear neither the physical world nor the knowledge of this world.

# Summary

All of the factors discussed above are significant in explaining why the greatest strides in modern science—from Plato and Aristotle, to early Christian and Jewish thinkers, to the golden era of Islam, to the explosion in scientific discovery among European Catholics and Protestants from the sixteenth to the eighteenth centuries—occurred when monotheistic thought was strongest and most dominant in the intellectual thinking of the day. Without the key contributions of monotheistic belief systems, it is unlikely that modern science and the research culture associated with it would have arisen in the form that it did. The implications of this are many, but two points merit specific mention.

Firstly, if the context created by monotheistic belief systems formed an environment conducive to the development of science, then these same developments in science and in scientific thinking also, in all likelihood, played a positive role in supporting the further development of robust and healthy expressions of monotheistic faith. The positive impact of significant phases in the rise of science on the monotheistic traditions in which these often occurred is an area that merits further research. The relationship between monotheism and science was not likely one of simple cause and effect, but one of complex mutuality in which each benefited in a variety of ways from the existence of the other. Science and monotheistic faith, distinct as their areas of competence might seem to be, have been healthiest and have thrived most when working in cooperation rather than in competition with one another.

Finally, recognising the role monotheism played in supporting the development of the modern scientific worldview, if more widely understood by Christians and other contemporary theists, would do much to counter the warfare model of the relationship between religion and science which has arisen over the course of the past century. It would also serve to foster a healthier dialogue between two important ways of thinking about the world that together have shaped the modern intellectual tradition.

Given the recent uneasy relationship between science and faith, science and monotheism would indeed appear to be unlikely allies. However, allies they have been, albeit often unwittingly, and allies they remain.

# Bibliography

Arieti, James and Patrick Wilson. *The Scientific and the Divine. Conflict and Reconciliation from Ancient Greece to the Present.* Oxford: Rowman and Littlefield, 2003.

Augustine. *The City of God.* Translated by C. D. Yonge. Peabody, MA: Hendrickson, 1993.

Barbour, Ian. *Religion and Science. Historical and Contemporary Issues.* Revised and expanded ed. London: SCM Press, 1998.

Brooke, John Hedley. *Science and Religion: Some Historical Perspectives.* Cambridge: Cambridge University Press, 1991.

Buxton, Graham. *The Trinity, Creation and Pastoral Ministry. Imagining the Perichoretic God.* Milton Keynes, UK: Paternoster, 2005.

Carrier, Richard. "Christianity Was Not Responsible for Modern Science." In *The Christian Delusion. Why Faith Fails*, edited by John Loftus. Amherst, NY: Prometheus Books, 2010: 396–419.

Chalmers, A. F. *What Is This Thing Called Science?* 3rd ed. Brisbane: University of Queensland Press, 1999.

Cormack, Lesley. "Myth 3: That Medieval Christians Taught That the Earth Was Flat." In *Galileo Goes to Jail and Other Myths about Science and Faith*, edited by Ronald Numbers. Cambridge, MA: Harvard University Press, 2009.

Coyne, Jerry. "Did Christianity (and Other Religions) Promote the Rise of Science?" *Why Evolution in True* (blog), October 18, 2019. https://whyevolutionistrue.wordpress.com/2013/10/18/did-christianity-and-other-religions-promote-the-rise-of-science/.

D'Souza, Dinesh. *What's So Great About Christianity.* Chicago: Tyndale, 2008.

Darwin, Charles. *The Origin of Species* [1859]. London: J. M. Dent & Sons, 1928.

de Santillana, Georgio. *The Origin of Scientific Thought from Anaximander to Proclus, 600BC–500AD.* Chicago: University of Chicago Press, 1961.

Deason, Gary. "Reformation Theology and the Mechanistic Conception of Nature." In *God and Nature: Historical Essays on the Encounter Between Christianity and Science*, edited by David Lindberg and Ronald Numbers. Berkeley: University of California Press, 1986.

Dillenberger, John. *Protestant Thought and Natural Science. A Historical Study*. London: Collins, 1961.

Draper, John William. *History of the Conflict Between Religion and Science*. London: Henry S. King, 1875.

Efron, Noah. "Myth 9: That Christianity Gave Birth to Modern Science." In *Galileo Goes to Jail and Other Myths about Science and Faith*, edited by Ronald Numbers. Cambridge, MA: Harvard University Press, 2009.

El-Mahassni, Edwin. "Kuhn's Structural Revolutions and the Development of Christian Doctrine: A Systematic Discussion." *Heythrop Journal* 59, no. 3 (May 2018): 509–522.

Finocchiaro, Maurice. "Myth 8: That Galileo Was Imprisoned and Tortured for Advocating Copernicanism." In *Galileo Goes to Jail and Other Myths about Science and Faith*, edited by Ronald Numbers. Cambridge, MA: Harvard University Press, 2009.

Funkenstein, Amos. *Theology and the Scientific Imagination from the Middle Ages to the Seventeenth Century*. Princeton, NJ: Princeton University Press, 1986.

Haq, Syed Nomanul, "Moments in the Islamic Recasting of the Greek Legacy: Exploring the Question of Science and Theism." In *God, Life, and the Cosmos: Christian and Islamic Perspectives,* edited by T. Peters, M. Iqbal, and S. Haq. Aldershot, UK: Ashgate 2002.

Haq, Syed Nomanul. "Myth 4: That Medieval Islamic Culture Was Inhospitable to Science." In *Galileo Goes to Jail and Other Myths about Science and Faith*, edited by Ronald Numbers. Cambridge, MA: Harvard University Press, 2009.

Harrison, Peter. *The Bible, Protestantism, and the Rise of Natural Science*. Cambridge, UK: Cambridge University Press, 1998.

Hassan, Hassan. "Don't blame it on al-Ghazali." *Qauntara.de* (2013). https://en.qantara.de/content/the-decline-of-islamic-scientific-thought-dont-blame-it-on-al-ghazali.

Haught, John. *God After Darwin. A Theology of Evolution*. Boulder, CO: Westview Press, 2000.

Hill, Christopher. *The Intellectual Origins of the English Revolution*. Oxford: Clarendon Press, 1965.

Hooykaas, R. *Religion and the Rise of Modern Science*. Edinburgh: Scottish Academic Press, 1972.

Hoyle, Fred. *Nicolas Copernicus: An Essay on His Life and Work*. London: Heinemann, 1973.

Isaacson, Walter. *Einstein: His Life and Universe*. New York: Simon & Schuster, 2007.

Jaki, Stanley. *The Road of Science and the Ways to God*. Chicago: University of Chicago Press, 1978.

Jellie, W. H. "Draper's 'Religion and Science.'" *Dickinson's Theological Quarterly* 3 (1877): 150–154.

Karras, Valerie. "Orthodoxy and Science in the Fourth Century." In *Science and the Eastern Orthodox Church*, edited by Daniel Buxhoeveden and Gayle Woloschak. Aldershot, UK: Ashgate, 2011.

Knight, David. *Copernicus*. London: Franklin Watts, 1965.

Kuhn, Thomas. *The Structure of Scientific Revolutions*, 2nd enlarged ed. Chicago: University of Chicago Press, 1970.

Le Coz, R. *Les médecins nestoriens au Moyen Âge: Les maîtres des Arabes*. Paris: L'Harmattan, 2004.

Libby, Walter. *An Introduction to the History of Science*. Boston: Houghton Mifflin, 1917.

Livingstone, David. *Darwin's Forgotten Defenders: The Encounter between Evangelical Theology and Evolutionary Thought*. Grand Rapids: Eerdmans, 1987.

Mason, Stephen. *A History of the Sciences*. New York: Macmillan, 1962.

Mendel, Gregor. "Versuche über Pflanzenhybriden." In *Verhandlungen des naturforschenden Vereines in Brünn* 4 (1866):1–47.

Merton, Robert K. "Science, Technology, and Society in 17th-Century England." *Osiris* 4 (1938): 360–632.

Moore, James. *The Post-Darwinian Controversies. A Study of the Protestant Struggle To Come to Terms with Darwin in Great Britain and America 1870–1900*. Cambridge: Cambridge University Press, 1979.

Nagamia, Husain. "Pioneers of Islamic Medicine series no. 2: The Bukhtishus." International Institute of Islamic Medicine (website). http://www.iiim.org/Files/Bukhtishu/The_Bukhtishu%27s.pdf

Nebelsick, Harold. *Circles of God: Theology and Science from the Greeks to Copernicus*. Edinburgh: Scottish Academic Press, 1985.

Nebelsick, Harold. *The Renaissance, the Reformation and the Rise of Science*. Edinburgh: T&T Clark, 1992.

Newton, Isaac. *Principia: The Mathematical Principles of Natural Philosophy* [1687]. Translated by Andrew Mott. Amherst: Prometheus Books, 1995.

Niebuhr, H. Richard. *Radical Monotheism and Western Culture, With Supplementary Essays*. New York: Harper and Brothers, 1960.

Numbers, Ronald. *The Creationists: The Evolution of Scientific Creationism*. New York: Alfred Knopf, 1992.

Ofek, Hillel. "Why the Arabic World Turned Away from Science." *The New Atlantis* 30 (Winter 2011): 3–23.

Pannenberg, Wolfhart. "Theological Questions to Scientists." In *The Sciences and Theology in the Twentieth Century*, edited by A. Peacocke. Notre Dame: University of Notre Dame Press 1981.

Pormann, Peter and Emilie Savage-Smith. *Medieval Islamic Medicine*. Washington: Georgetown University Press, 2007.

Powell, Samuel. *Participating in God. Creation and Trinity*. Minneapolis: Fortress Press, 2003.

Ruse, Michael. *The Evolution-Creation Struggle*. Cambridge, MA: Harvard University Press, 2006.

Sarton, George. *Ancient Science and Modern Civilization*. New York: Harper & Brothers, 1954.

Saud, Muhammad. *The Scientific Method of Ibn Al-Hyatham*. Islamabad: Islamic Research Institute, 1990.

Schwarz, Hans. *The Search for God: Christianity – Atheism – Secularism – World Religions*. Minneapolis: Augsburg, 1975.

Spanier, David. *Total Chess*. New York: Penguin, 1984.

Stark, Rodney. *For the Glory of God. How Monotheism Led to Reformations, Science, Witch Hunts and the End of Slavery*. Princeton, NJ: Princeton University Press, 2004.

Tirosh-Samuelson, Hava. "Nature in the Sources of Judaism." *Daedalus* 130, no. 4 (September 2011): 99–124

Torrance, T. F. *Reality and Scientific Theology*. Edinburgh: Scottish Academic Press, 1985.

Turner, Harold. *The Roots of Science: An Investigative Journey through the World's Religions*. Auckland: Deepsight Trust, 1998.

Weber, Max. *Ancient Judaism*. New York: Free Press, 1952.

Weber, Max. *Gesammelte Aufsätze zur Relgionssoziologie*. Vol I. Tübingen: J.C.B. Mohr, 1923.

Webster, Charles. *The Great Instauration: Science, Medicine and Reform 1626–1660*. London: Duckworth, 1975.

White, Andrew Dickson. *A History of the Warfare of Science with Theology in Christendom*. New York: D. Appleton and Company, 1896.

Whitehead, Alfred North. *Science and the Modern World*. Cambridge: Cambridge University Press, 1926.

Worthing, Mark. "Luther on the Border of Superstition and Science" In *Martin Luther. A Wild Boar in the Lord's Vineyard*. Melbourne: Morning Star, 2017.

Worthing, Mark. "Some brief reflections on Christology and the Natural Sciences." *Lutheran Theological Journal* 47, no. 1. (May 2013): 4–9.

Worthing, Mark. "Theology and Science: A Brief History." In *God and Science in Classroom and Pulpit*, by G. Buxton, C. Mulherin and M. Worthing. Revised ed. Melbourne: Morning Star, 2018.

Worthing, Mark. *God, Creation, and Contemporary Physics*. Minneapolis: Fortress Press, 1996.

Worthing, Mark. *Nestorian Christian Contributions to Medicine and Science in the Golden Age of Islam under the Abbasid Caliphs of Baghdad 786–1258 CE*. Melbourne: Morning Star, forthcoming.